Little
Science
Stars

Light
and Sound

The Best Start in Science

By Clint Twist

ticktock

ISBN-13: 978 1 84898 061 7 pbk
This revised edition published in 2009 by *ticktock* Media Ltd

Printed in China
9 8 7 6 5 4 3 2 1

Copyright © *ticktock* Entertainment Ltd 2005
First published in Great Britain as *Check It Out!* in 2005 by *ticktock* Media Ltd,
The Old Sawmill, 103 Goods Station Road, Tunbridge Wells, Kent, TN1 2DP

Picture credits (t=top, b=bottom, c=centre, l=left, r=right,
OFC=outside front cover, OBC=outside back cover):

Corbis: 12b, 13t, 18t, 20 all, 22l. Powerstock: 10t, 10b, 17 all, 18b, 21t.
Shutterstock: OFC all, 1 all, 2, 3 all, 4–5 all, 6–7 all, 9b, 10–11b, 11 all, 12t both, 14 all, 15 all, 16 all, 19 all, 21b, 22b, 22–23 (background), 23 all, 24 all, OBC both.
ticktock Media Archive: 8–9, 13b.

Every effort has been made to trace the copyright holders and we apologize in advance for any unintentional omissions. We would be pleased to insert the appropriate acknowledgements in any subsequent edition of this publication.

Contents

Any words appearing in the text in bold, **like this**, are explained in the Glossary.

Light and sound are all
around us every day.
Without light and sound
we would not be able
to see or hear.

Cock-a-
doodle-doo

Bright light

Shouting

Loud noise

Light and **sound** are both
types of energy.

Light is energy that we
see with our eyes.
Sound is energy that we
hear with our ears.

Where does light come from?

The main way we get light on **Earth** is from the **Sun**.
We call this light **sunlight**.

NEVER look
directly at the Sun,
even if you are
wearing sunglasses,
because it can
damage
your eyes.

Sunlight is very **bright**
when there are no **clouds**.
Bright light helps us to see
things easily.

Clouds

Clouds in the sky
sometimes block
out some of the
sunlight.

The clouds make the sunlight **dim**, or less bright.
It can be harder to see when the light is dim.

Sunflower

Without sunlight, plants, animals and people could not live.

Plants need sunlight to help them grow. They use sunlight to make a special food inside themselves.

Without plants, animals and people could not live.
We need plants for food.

Why does it get dark at night?

When there is no light, there is **darkness**.

Sun

There is darkness at night because one half of Earth blocks out the Sun's light from the other half.

Our Earth is a big spinning ball. It takes 24 hours to spin all the way round.

A **day** and a night last 24 hours.

As your part of the Earth spins away from the Sun it gets dark. We call this **night**.

Light = Day

Dark = Night

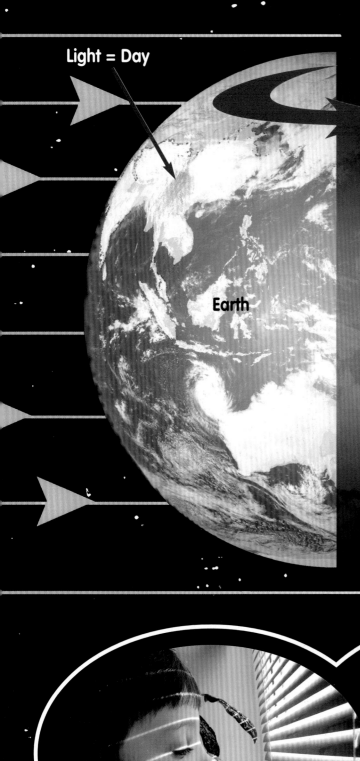

Earth

When we block the light it makes darkness in the room.

There are lots of ways to block light. We use blinds or curtains to block light at our windows.

How do we see when it's dark?

When it's dark we can make **artificial light**.

We can switch on a lamp to make light.

The light is brightest close to the lamp. The light gets dimmer further away from the lamp.

Dimmer light

We can make artificial light by switching on a torch, too.

The closer you hold the torch to the book, the easier it is to see the words.

At night, drivers switch on their car headlights to light up the road.

At night, we switch on lights in houses, shops and offices. We use a type of energy called **electricity** to power the lights.

House

Shops

Offices

REMEMBER
Don't waste electricity!
Switch off the light
when you leave a room.

How does light travel?

Light travels in straight lines. This means we cannot see around corners or over walls.

We cannot see who is behind the tree...

...or what's inside the box.

The dog cannot see the cat because the wall blocks any light travelling between them.

But if the cat jumps up on the wall, light can travel between them.

Now the dog can see the cat!

If light shines through a shaped hole it will keep the same shape as the hole.

This is because light travels in a straight line unless it is blocked.

What is sound?

Sound is tiny shaking movements of the **air**. We call these tiny movements **vibrations**.

If you drop a pebble into water, you will see little waves spread out.

Waves

Sound vibrations move through the air in the same way.

We cannot feel or see the vibrations, but our ears are designed to detect them.

Our ears pick up the vibrations, then our brain turns them into sounds that we know.

Ears

An animal's ears work in the same way as your ears.

What makes sounds loud and quiet?

Sounds travel away from the things that made them. As they travel away, they get faint, or quiet.

Drums

The sound of these drums is loud if you are close to them.

If you are far away the sound is quieter.

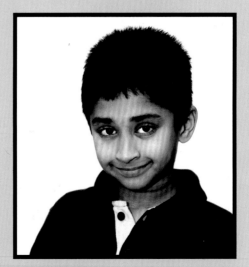

We can make loud sounds and quiet sounds.

A whisper is a quiet sound. When we whisper we can only be heard by people near to us.

Shouting is a loud sound.

We shout when we want someone far away to hear us.

A shout is very loud if you are near to the person who is shouting.

How do we make sounds?

This boy is plucking the guitar strings. They vibrate and make sounds that we call music.

Guitar

When the guitar strings stop vibrating, the music stops.

Hitting the top of a drum makes it vibrate and produce sound.

Hitting the drum gently makes a quiet sound. Hitting it hard makes a loud sound.

18

We use our voices to make singing sounds.

We can use our hands to make clapping sounds.

Animals make sounds too.

Hoowwwlllll

Baa Baa

Hello there!

Some parrots learn to make sounds like people!

Can we block out sound?

Sound travels through the air in a different way to light. Sound is not as easy to block as light.

The cat cannot see the dog, but she can hear him barking.

This mother cat cannot see her kitten, but she can hear it miaowing.

You can hear this fire engine's siren as it speeds by.

If the fire engine goes around a corner,
you will still be able to hear the siren!

We can stop our ears
picking up the sound
of the siren by
covering them.

REMEMBER
Don't ever stick
things in your
ears!

Questions and answers

Q Can dogs hear better than people?

A Yes, they can! Dogs can hear sounds that are too quiet for us to hear. They can also hear sounds that are a long way away. Dogs can move their ears in different directions to pick up sounds.

Q How many different sounds can you hear in your home or garden?

A Here are some to get you started:
- TV
- Radio
- Vacuum cleaner
- Telephone
- Birds
- Lawnmower

Look around and listen. Some sounds are loud and some are very quiet.

Q Can loud noises hurt your ears?

A Yes, they can, so protect your ears. Don't turn the music up too loud if you are wearing headphones.

Q What artificial light did people use before electricity was invented?

A They used candles.

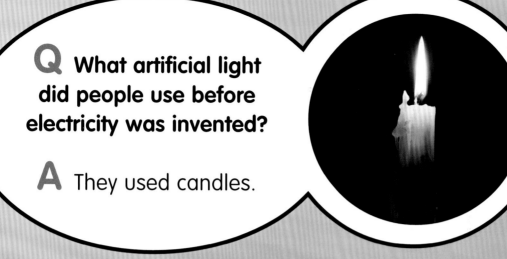

Q How fast do sound vibrations travel through the air?

A They travel at over 1,200 kilometres per hour.

Q What is the fastest thing in the world?

A Light is the fastest thing in our world. Light energy travels in waves at 300,000 kilometres per hour.

Q What sound in your home can save you from danger?

A The smoke alarm. Make sure a grown-up checks the alarm every month.

Glossary

Air A mixture of gases that are all around us on the Earth's surface. People and animals breathe air.

Artificial light Light that is made by humans such as through lamps or torches.

Bright Easy to see.

Clouds Clusters of water droplets that float in the air.

Darkness When there is no light.

Day The hours when we have daylight from morning to evening.

Dim Difficult to see.

Earth The planet where we live. Earth is a huge, ball of rock. The Earth is always spinning.

Electricity A type of energy that we use to make light and heat and to power machines.

Light A type of energy that we see with our eyes.

Night The hours when it is dark from evening to morning.

Sound A type of energy that we hear with our ears.

Sun The Sun is a star, just like the ones we see twinkling in the sky at night. The Sun is closer to the Earth than any other star so we can feel heat from it.

Sunlight Light that comes from the Sun during the day.

Vibrations Tiny movements that happen when something shakes backwards and forwards, or from side to side, very quickly.

Index